COLLAGE

Hilary Devonshire

Photography: Chris Fairclough

FRANKLIN WATTS
London/New York/Sydney/Toronto

Franklin Watts Inc.
387 Park Avenue South,
New York, NY 10016

ISBN: 0-531-10556-3
Library of Congress
Catalog Card
No: 87-51703

Design: Edward Kinsey

Editor: Jenny Wood

Printed in Belgium

The author wishes to record her thanks in the preparation of this book to: Henry Pluckrose for his advice and guidance; Christopher Fairclough for the excellence of his step-by-step photographs; Anne Clark for the loan of her pressed flower pictures; Emma Tingle for her picture, "Map of Denmark"; and Chester Fisher, Franklin Watts Ltd.

Contents

This book describes activities that use the following:

Blotting paper
Brushes for glue and paint
Compass (for drawing circles)
Thread
Crayons
Fabrics (assorted scraps e.g. canvas, cotton, felt, fur, burlap, lace, netting, nylon, ribbon, silk, velvet)
Felt-tip pen
Glue – clear, cold water past (Pritt Art Paste, clear/wallpaper paste white glue such as Elmer's or Sabo)
Jar for mixing paste
Junk materials (buttons, corks, labels, lids, matchsticks, net bags, plastic, raffia, sequins, aluminum foil, straw, paper wrappings, yogurt cartons)
Knife
Marbling colors
Materials from nature (e.g. bark, feathers, flowers, grasses, leaves, pine cones, seeds, egg shells, sea shells, twigs)
Newspapers and magazines

Palette knife (or wooden spatula)
Paper – hard paper: cardboard, such as posterboard or oaktag (thin), and Bristolboard or railroad board (thick), medium weight white drawing paper, corrugated cardboard, construction paper, postcards – soft thin paper: gummed sheets, tissue papers, transparent colored papers such as cellophane, typing paper
Paper clips
Paper towels.
Pencil
Plaster of Paris
Postage stamps (used)
Powder paints
Ruler
Sand
Saucer or plate (old) for mixing plaster
Scissors
String
Telephone directory (or heavy book)
Water
Yarn

Collage is a way of making pictures by gluing different materials, objects or shapes onto a background support. The word "collage" comes from a French word, "coller", which means 'to glue.' It is exciting to experiment with all the different materials you can use.

In this book you will find many ideas for collage work. The materials do not have to be expensive, and you will probably already have many of them in your home – unwanted bits and pieces tucked away in cupboards and drawers. I hope that when you have read this book you will want to experiment and try some of the ideas for yourself.

If you become a collage enthusiast you will want to hoard all sorts of materials such as scraps of fabric, assorted "junk," old magazines and newspapers, buttons and bits of wood.

1 Important pieces of equipment.

Some hints

It is a good idea to store your collection in a large box. Keep the smaller objects in clear plastic bags so that you can easily see and select the ones you need.

The adhesives you use will depend upon the type and weight of material or object you are sticking. Most work can be done with a light adhesive, although heavy items will need thicker, stronger glue.

Collage work can be messy. Before you start, remember to cover the table and floor with newspaper.

You will also need an apron, or a large, old shirt or blouse to protect your clothes.

2 A selection of "hard" papers.

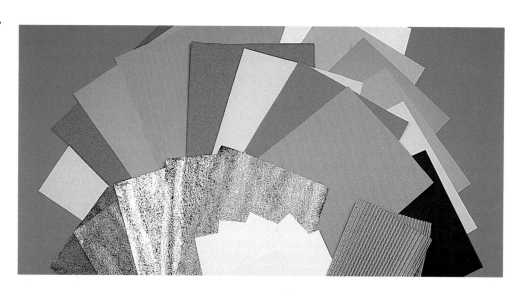

3 A selection of "soft" papers.

All kinds of paper are suitable for paper collage. You can use soft or hard papers, and these can be either cut or torn to create a picture or design.

Use a clear paste (e.g. Pritt Art Paste), and hard paper (e.g. construction paper) for mounting.

1 *Landscape*
A collage made from an assortment of colored paper scraps. Notice that pieces of paper are laid over each other to create a design.

Tissue paper collage

For this idea you will need a
selection of coloured tissue
papers, clear paste (e.g. Pritt Art
Paste), and a glue brush.

1 Tissue paper is easy
to tear into shapes.
Torn paper gives a
better effect for
natural designs such
as trees and
landscapes; cut paper
is best for man-made
objects such as
buildings or ships.

2 *Country Scene*
The different tissue
papers can give subtle
variations of color
where they overlap,
because the thin tissue
is translucent.

Marbled paper collage

You will need some marbled sheets of paper, (patterned papers made with thinned oil colors – see the book on *Paints* in this series), some black construction paper, glue and a glue brush, scissors, and hard paper (e.g. construction paper).

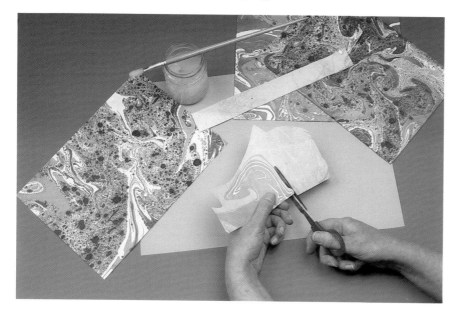

1 The colors and patterns of the marbled papers may suggest the subject of your picture. Here waves are being cut from the swirls in the patterns.

2 A ship silhouette is cut from the black construction paper and arranged among the waves.

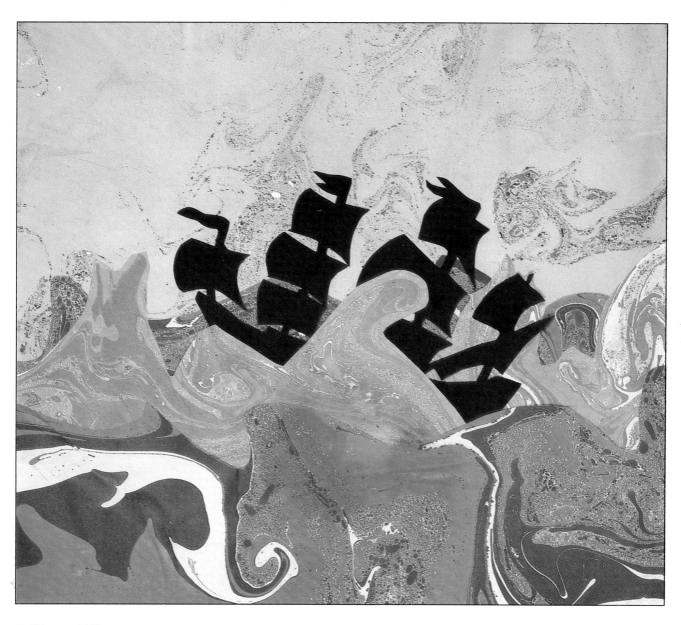

3 *Storm At Sea*
The finished picture.

Newspaper, like tissue paper, is easy to tear.

Tear out some paper figures. It is fun to make them run and jump by bending their arms and legs.

Besides newspapers, you will need glue and a glue brush, and hard paper (e.g. construction paper) in a dark color.

1 Fold a sheet of newspaper. Tear half a figure along the fold.

2 You will need to tear out a number of figures if you want to form a crowd.

3 *The Football Game* Glue the arms and legs down bending them any way you want to show action. The dark paper mount gives a contrasting background to your figures.

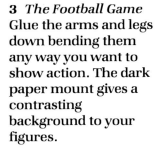

Stamp mosaics

Mosaics are small colored pieces which can be fitted together to make a pattern or picture. Long ago the Greeks and Romans used pebbles or pieces of colored glass or tile to make mosaic pictures.

The following pages (12–17) will give you ideas for using paper mosaics in different ways.

Postage stamps can be used as ready-made mosaics. Make a collection of old stamps and sort them by color. You can remove stamps from envelopes by soaking them in water for a short time.

You will also need paper, a crayon or felt-tip pen, clear paste (e.g. Elmer's glue thinned with water), and a glue brush.

1 Draw a picture on a sheet of paper.

2 Stick the stamps on to your design.

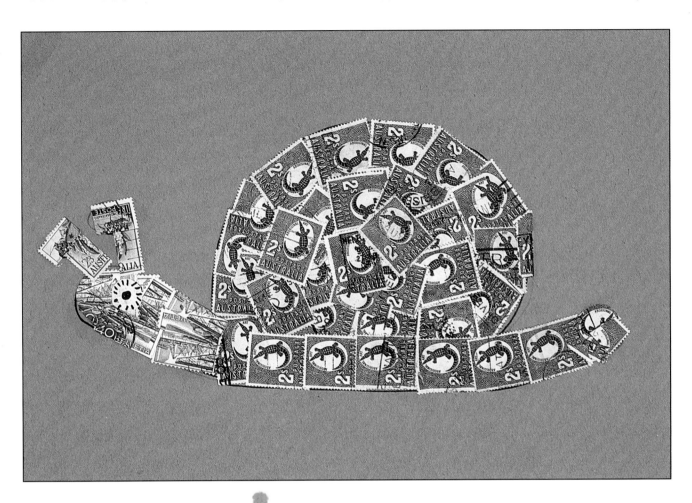

3 *Snail*
The finished picture.

Torn paper mosaics

You will need different colored papers, a sheet of hard paper (such as construction paper) on which to arrange your picture, a pencil, glue and a glue brush.

1 Tear some colored paper into small pieces. Draw a design on the sheet of hard paper. First arrange, and then glue the small pieces of paper (the mosaics) onto the sheet of hard paper to complete your picture.

2 (Below) *The Pike* The background has also been colored with a mosaic design

3 (Right) *Map of Denmark* Made by a Danish schoolgirl.

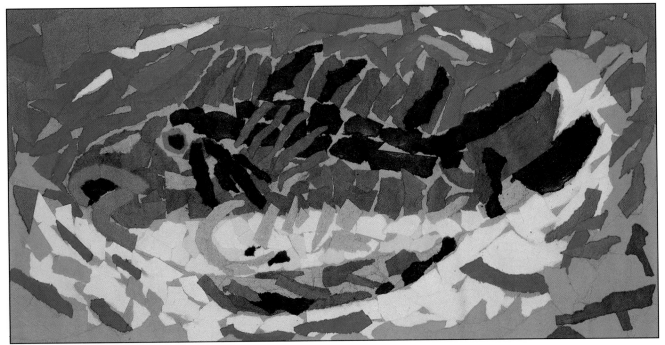

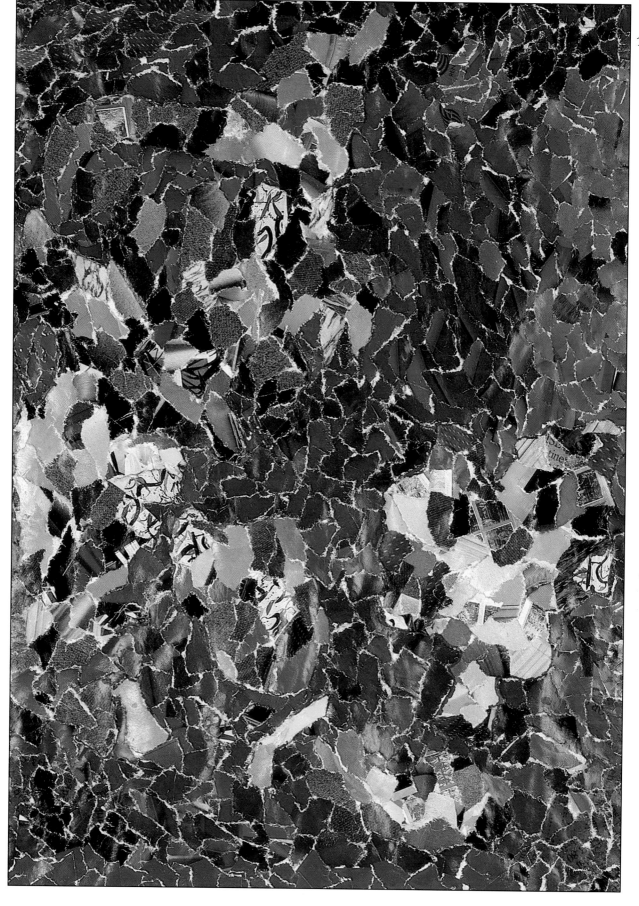

Alphabet mosaics

You will need newspapers and magazines, scissors, a crayon or felt-tip pen, a sheet of hard paper (such as construction paper), glue and a glue brush.

1 Draw a picture on to the sheet of hard paper. Can you decorate it using only the initial letter of the name of the object in the picture? Cut as many versions of this letter as you can from the magazines.

2 (Right) *The Train* Lorraine has used the letter T to decorate her train. The background has been painted black to make the train stand out.

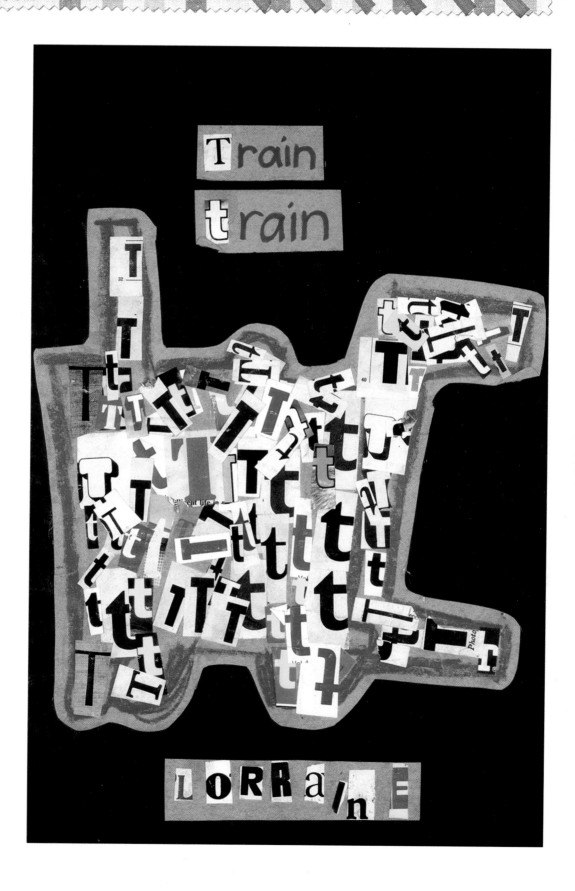

In this technique, a picture or shape is cut into different pieces and the pieces rearranged with spaces in between to give a new, extended picture. Remember that all the pieces must be used – no pieces are thrown away. The results can often be very surprising!

You will need a picture, a pencil, a ruler, scissors, glue and a glue brush, and a sheet of paper on which to mount the new picture.

1 First, choose your picture.

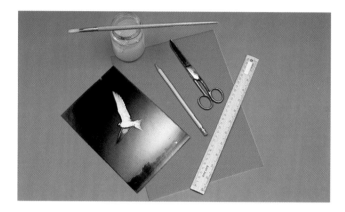

2 Draw lines on the back of the picture to show where you are going to cut.

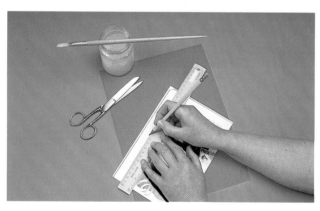

3 Cutting the picture.

4 *Flight*
The picture has been arranged and then glued onto the sheet of paper, giving a completely new image.

5 *Gorilla*
How much bigger he
looks!

You will need two sheets of paper in contrasting colors, a felt-tip pen, scissors, glue and a glue brush.

1 Cut a circle from one piece of paper, and fold it in half.

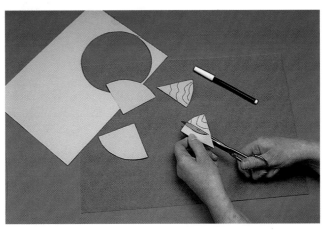

2 Fold and cut the circle into quarters. Cut each quarter into smaller pieces.

3 The small pieces can be arranged in many ways. Experiment with your pattern before sticking the pieces down.

4 *Exploding Circle*
Could you use this idea starting
with a square, triangle or
hexagon?

These designs are another form of extended picture. You will need papers of contrasting colors.

For this technique different shapes are cut out. The shapes, and their cut-away spaces, are then arranged and mounted on a contrasting background to give a reflected or repeated pattern.

For this idea you will need a sheet of white paper, one square sheet of black gummed paper, a compass, pencil, scissors, clear paste (e.g. wallpaper paste), and a glue brush.

1 Fold and cut the gummed square in half. Cut a few shapes from one side of each half.

2 Arrange the shapes so that they lie opposite and reflect the space from which they were cut. Stick them down with the clear paste.

3 The finished design.

You will need sheets of paper in contrasting colors, glue and a glue brush, a pencil, scissors, and paper clips.

1 Draw your design on one of the sheets of paper. A useful hint is to make a cardboard template of your design. This will enable you to repeat it many times.

2 Cut out the design. Here the design has been cut from both blue and yellow paper. You can arrange the shapes and their cut-away images in many ways. Experiment to obtain a pleasing pattern before sticking down the final design.

3 The pattern can be reflected, rotated and repeated.

4 (Below) Here the design has been overlapped. Could you make a circular design in the same way?

Many different materials can be used for fabric collage. Fabrics give a greater thickness and variety of texture than paper in collage work.

Use a large box in which to keep all sorts of fabric samples or scraps of material. Try to collect a wide variety, such as smooth velvets and silks, brightly colored cottons and nylons; heavier felts, canvas, and burlap to give rough, uneven surfaces and textures; and an assortment of bits of ribbon, netting, lace trimmings, yarn and string.

1 A selection of fabrics suitable for fabric collage.

2 For your collage work you will need scissors, some heavy cardboard, an assortment of fabrics, glue and a glue brush. White PVA glue is good for sticking fabric as it becomes transparent when dry.

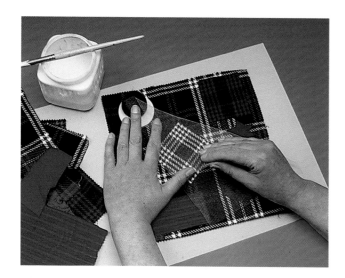

3 Cut and arrange your materials to give a pleasing design before sticking. Remember that you can glue one piece of fabric on top of another.

4 The finished collage. The two thick felt circles support the netting and give a depth to the design.

Yarn and string collage

You will need cardboard, a pencil, string, yarn, glue and a glue brush.

1 The design of the frog was first drawn on cardboard and then outlined with string. Yarn is being used to decorate the body.

2 The finished collage. Yarn flowers are added to complete the picture.

Plaster collage

You will need some heavy paper or thin cardboard, a dark colored crayon, some plaster of Paris (and water to mix), an old saucer or plate and a wooden spatula or palette knife.

1 First draw the outline of your picture with the crayon. Then mix the plaster to a thick, creamy consistency. Using the palette knife or spatula, carefully spread the plaster within the outline. You will have to work quite fast since the plaster will begin to set as you work.

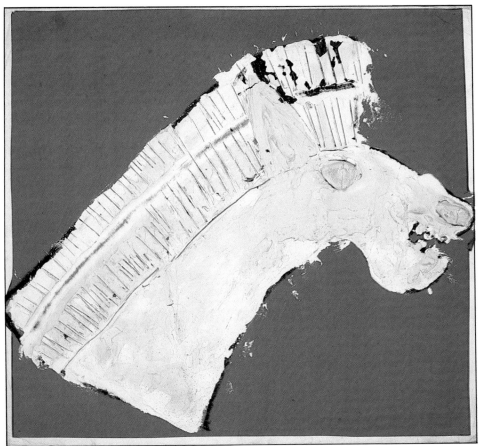

2 *Greek Horse* (From the Elgin Marbles) The features, such as hair and eyes, have been created by drawing into or building up the thickness of the plaster.

You will need cardboard, a pencil, sand, white glue and a glue brush, and a sheet of paper.

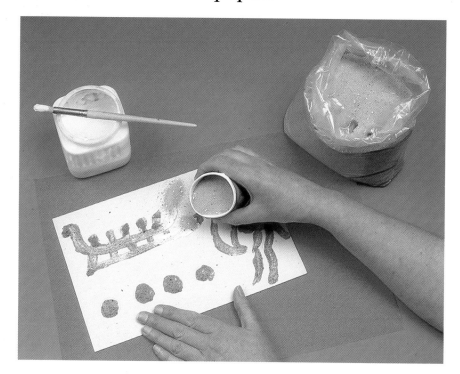

1 Draw the outline of your design on the cardboard in pencil and fill it in with glue. Sprinkle sand over the glue. It is easier to work a small section at a time while the glue is still wet.

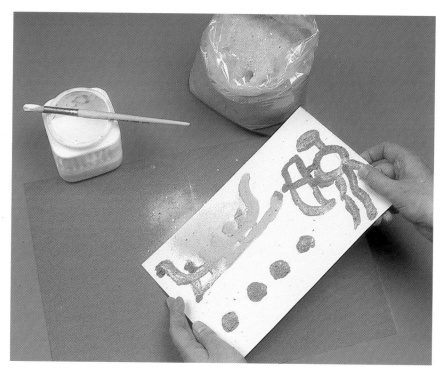

2 Shake any surplus sand carefully onto the sheet of paper. If you fold the paper down the middle it is easy to pour the unused sand along the fold, back into the bag.

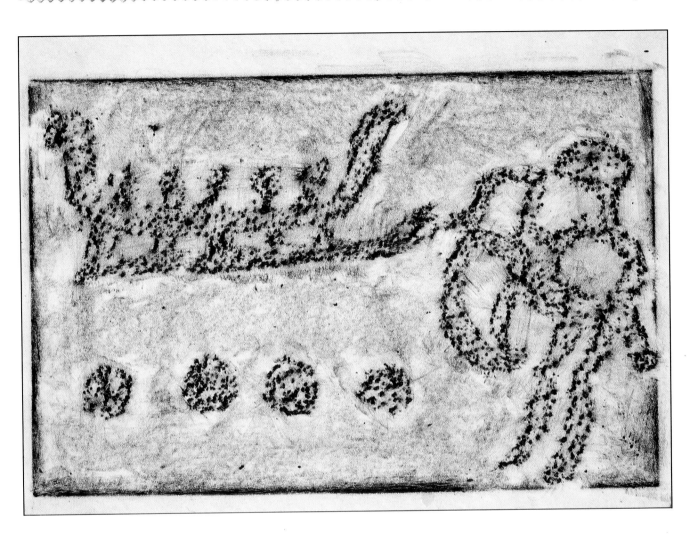

3 *Swedish Rock Carving*
When it was dry, the finished
sand design was used to take a
crayon rubbing (see the book
on *Crayons* in this series).

All kinds of throw-away objects can be used for collage work. The following two ideas (pages 33 and 34) make use of old buttons and corks.

For this type of collage you will need heavy cardboard, white glue and a glue brush.

Collect buttons from old clothes that are about to be thrown away.

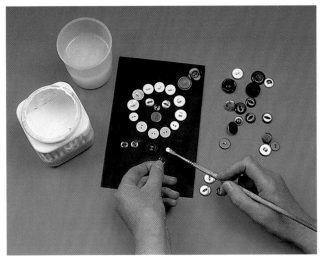

1 (Above) Experiment with arranging the buttons before starting to glue.

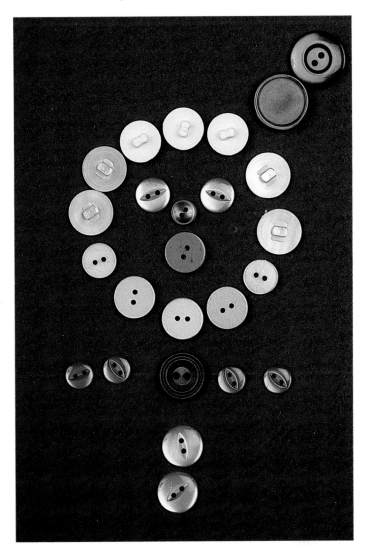

2 (Left) *Button Man*
The black cardboard contrasts with the shiny buttons.

Cork collage

You will need heavy cardboard, some old corks, a knife, white glue and a glue brush.

1 Cut the corks into different lengths. Arrange them on the cardboard to create a design in depth.

2 The finished cork design. Interesting three-dimensional work can be achieved. Can you tell that the corks are different lengths when viewed from above?

An assemblage is a collage created from more than one type of material. Pictures designed in this way are often three-dimensional, with projecting materials or objects that give the picture thickness and depth. Finding the objects is fun; just use your imagination.

Your collection may be made from nature (e.g. pine cones, seeds, dried leaves, twigs, seashells, feathers or egg shells). Or you can use bits of junk. Experiment with objects no longer needed for their original purpose (e.g. net bags made for holding fruit at the supermarket, old labels, yogurt cartons, lids or candy wrappers). Making an assemblage is a creative way of using "unusable" items.

Once you have made your collection you are ready to start.

You will also need some heavy cardboard for mounting, white glue and a glue brush.

1 (Above) Materials from nature.

2 (Left) "Junk" materials.

Nature collage: Glazing

Here are two ways of making and preserving plants from nature.

For glazing you need a collection of leaves and grasses, some white glue diluted with water to make a glaze, a brush, and paper.

First cover a sheet of paper with a layer of glaze. Arrange your design of leaves and grasses on the glazed paper. Remember this will be very sticky.

Cover your design with glaze, making sure you have covered all of the surface of the plants to exclude the air. Leave to dry.

You will find that your picture dries shiny, and that your leaves and grasses will be preserved for a long time.

1 The finished picture.

This method takes time and care. It is suitable for handling and preserving delicate flowers and grasses. (Remember, some wild flowers are protected species.)

Collect your flowers, petals, leaves, or grasses, and place them flat between two sheets of newspaper or blotting paper. Press them between the pages of a heavy book, such as a telephone directory, for about 4–6 weeks.

Handle the pressed flowers very carefully. Arrange them on a piece of cardboard. Stick them down with a tiny amount of white glue.

If you like, you can cover your design with a transparent adhesive paper to protect them from damage.

1 *Flower Garden*

2 Framed, pressed
flowers make
attractive gifts.

Collage from assorted materials

For this technique you will need your *Whole* collection of materials, then you can see what ideas for picture-making they suggest to you.

In the following pictures a variety of materials has been used.

1 (Above) Tissue paper can be crumpled into small pieces and used to fill in a section of a picture. Here the face is being colored.

2 (Left) *Nurse* (by a 6-year-old) Tissue paper, gummed paper squares, yarn and paints have been incorporated.

3 Plastic rings become the eyes, and striped plastic bags make the jacket of this scarecrow.

4 *Scarecrow*
What other materials have been used for this picture?

Now that you have used this book, you have worked and experimented with many different kinds of materials. You have also discovered how the different adhesives behave.

Here are some more ideas and suggestions for you to try.

1 Try to make a picture that combines two or more of the ideas contained in this book. For example, you could make a marbled paper collage of the ocean with a sand collage beach.

2 Glaze a tissue paper collage. This will give the picture a shiny finish (see photograph 1).

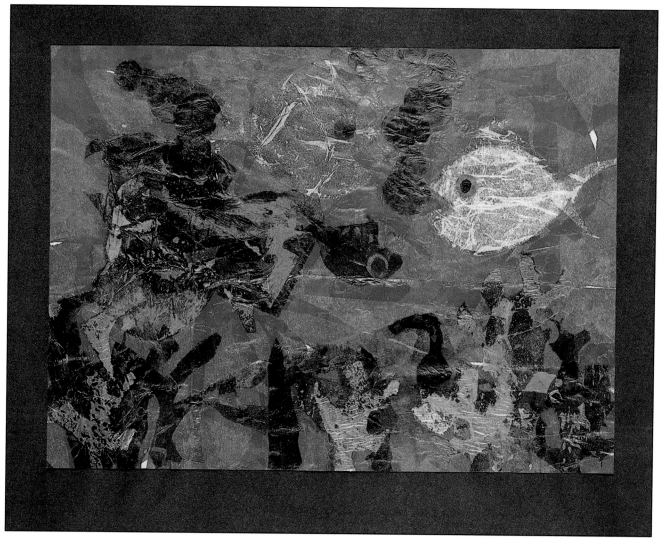

1 *Underwater Scene*

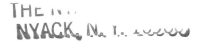

3 Make a collage using hard
paper. You may then be able to
print your picture (see
photographs **2** and **3**).

2 Troll

3 *Old Castle*

4 *Mask in red and blue*

4 Using the extended circle idea, make a book of different designs. You could ask your friends if they can recognise the shape you started with.

5 Make a mask with reflected shapes and colors using two gummed squares (see photograph **4**).

6 Decorate one of your paintings.
Collage can sometimes be used
on finished paintings. A picture
can often be enhanced in this
way (see photographs **5** and **6**).

5 *Flower Girl*
(by a 4-year old) Here,
cut-out flowers
decorate the picture.

6 *The Mermaid*
Sequins become the
shiny scales of the
mermaid's tail and the
jewels in her crown.

7 Make a three-dimensional
design. You will need thin
cardboard or oaktag, crayons,
assorted papers and materials,
scissors, thread, glue and a glue
brush (see photographs **7**, **8** and **9**).

7 Cut three pieces of
rectangular cardboard.
Draw a background
scene on one piece.
The remaining two will
become foreground
scenes.

8 (Left) In this three-
dimensional
underwater scene the
foreground contains a
treasure chest lying on
the sandy ocean bed,
and the central scene
shows a rocky setting.
"Marbled" fish hang
from the white frame.

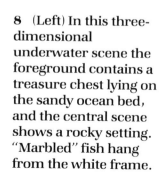

9 (Right) The three scenes are joined together on both sides by folded cardboard to make the picture free-standing.

Further information

Adhesives

Cold water paste (e.g. clear wallpaper paste or Pritt Art Paste) is suitable for sticking papers and lightweight materials. White glue (such as Elmer's) is suitable for heavier materials as well. It can also be thinned with water to make a glaze. Wallpaper paste and white glue (Elmer's or Sabo) can be purchased at hardware stores. *Impact adhesive should on no account be used.*

Paper and cardboard

Most stationers stock the papers and cardboard used in this book.

Materials from nature

Many natural materials such as autumn leaves, pine cones, shells, fallen bark and twigs, grasses and rose petals are abundant and freely available. *But remember that some species and specimens are rare and may not be picked or collected.*

Art Supplies

Art Supplies (or materials in large quantities) can be obtained from an art supply catalog, or ordered through a school supplier such as J. L. Hammett, Box 545, Hammett Place, Braintree, Mass. 02184.

Marbling colors

You can make your marbling colors using Hunt's Speedball Pro-Ink oil base or oil paints thinned with turpentine.